The Little Book Of

CLOUD COMPUTING SECURITY

2013 Edition

Lars Nielsen

2013
New Street Communications, LLC
Wickford, RI

newstreetcommunications.com

Published February 2013 by
New Street Communications, LLC
Wickford, Rhode Island
newstreetcommunications.com

Contents

Introduction

A word to the wise is infuriating.

– Hunter S. Thompson

Cloud computing security is easily *the* chief concern for both public (governmental) and private sector IT professionals. According to a recent study conducted by the The Computer Technology Industry Association, 44 percent of implementers stated that network security is the leading issue in adoption of Cloud computing. Specifically, issues preoccupying IT staff involve security mandate compliance (36 percent), data loss prevention (35 percent) and hardware security (35 percent).

Another survey conducted by NetIQ Corporation through Harris Interactive shows that 70 percent of respondents have been impacted by security breaches and still struggle to mitigate attacks due to limited time and resources. Fully 55 percent of respondents admit they lack the ability to manage security in virtualized and Cloud environments.

With organizations facing more challenges and risks than ever, IT security budgets continue to grow.

Nearly eight in ten (77 percent) respondents indicate IT security budgets are higher this year compared to last, and on average, over one-half (59 percent) of most enterprise IT budgets is allocated towards security.

White Clouds, Eugène Boudin, 1824-1898.

While 65 percent of respondents say they use an identity management solution, external and internal data theft remains high.

"We live in a data-driven society and access to sensitive or proprietary data continues to bleed past organizational walls, making it an ongoing challenge for IT security teams to protect corporate data," says Jay Roxe, Solution Marketing director, NetIQ.

"Organizations must be able to monitor activity across multiple environments, proactively identify and mitigate security threats in real time and allow for meaningful data analysis so that proactive controls can be implemented," Roxe continues. "By requiring these components, IT security teams can make better use of their resources, tackle the integration of new platforms and technologies and ultimately reduce organizational cost and risk."

My aim here is to provide lay readers with a concise, to-the-point, up-to-date, no-nonsense introduction to the fundamental security issues confronting those enterprises who have moved, or are considering a move, to the Cloud. I will explore both the advantages and the pitfalls of various options in order to provide the very best data by which enterprises can make informed decisions about how to proceed with their own Cloud security paradigm.

IT is currently in an important time of transition and consolidation *vis-a-vis* standards, protocols and best-practices for securing Cloud services and environments. Taking baby steps forward, we are making decisions today that will impact not just our individual firms, but our industries, for years to come. It is important that as individual enterprises, and as partners in larger endeavors, we get the foundations of Cloud security architected firmly and correctly, lest all our houses come crashing down some dark day in the future.

Lars Nielsen
Amsterdam, Holland

Shameless plugs: For a basic primer on the fundamentals of Cloud Computing, please take a look at my *Little Book of Cloud Computing*, which is updated annually. If you have an interest in how we got to where we are in business computing, consider my book *Computing: A Business History*. Others might find useful *A Simple Guide to Data Science*, which I've co-authored with Noreen Burlingame. Thus endeth my shameless plugs.

Fear and Loathing in the Cloud

The first rule of any technology used in a business is that automation applied to an efficient operation will magnify the efficiency. The second is that automation applied to an inefficient operation will magnify the inefficiency.

– Bill Gates

The peanut-counting accountants and managers in the front-offices of firms world-wide love the idea of the cost benefits offered by Cloud Computing. Many corporate IT security professionals, however, are not so enamored.

According to a recent industry survey conducted by Lieberman Software, approximately seven out of eight IT pros simply don't trust Cloud providers to effectively guard sensitive data,. (The survey also indicates that the majority of IT professionals do not trust Cloud providers with their own personal data.)

And guess what. Despite the exploits of the infamous *Anonymous*, the chief worry isn't cyber-criminals or hackers. The chief concern is a rogue employee at a Cloud service provider accessing data without authorization.

Why so much nervousness and distrust of Cloud vendors?

"The big problem is there is a lot of opaqueness in what Cloud providers do," says Philip Liberman, head of Lieberman Software. "Companies want transparency, access to audit log data, and visibility into internal controls that go beyond best practices."

Lieberman conducted his survey at a recent Cloud Security Alliance (CSA) Summit held November 2012. In the process, he gathered responses from 300 IT professionals. More than 70 percent of those surveyed represented firms with more than 1,000 employees; half represented firms with more than 5,000 employees.

Overall, there seems to be a total disconnect between Cloud providers and their customers (or potential customers) when it comes to the issues of security.

A recent study by the Ponemon Institute shows that more than two-thirds of IT managers place responsibility for *data* security with Cloud provider.s But a mere one-third of providers agree with this assessment.

A later Ponemon survey showed IT professionals nearly equally split over who should take responsibility for the security of *applications* in the Cloud: A third said Cloud providers most appropriately carry this burden; a third defined security as a shared responsibility; and just a bit less than a third said they themselves were responsible for the security of apps in the Cloud.

According to the CSA's John Howie, while enterprises are slowly gaining trust in Cloud providers, the process drags because most Cloud providers have thus far failed to enable visibility into their security measures; and most IT managers don't like the idea of surrendering their sensitive data to a black-box.

Via the Security, Trust and Assurance Registry (STAR) – detailed in a later chapter – the CSA has sought to facilitate the needed transparency.

More, however, is necessary. Consensus says that what's needed is a carefully-crafted combo of certifications, standards, and audit reports contrived to give Cloud customers the info they need to gauge a provider's security – *all done without giving away too many details about security measures to potential attackers.* The CSA and others are currently at work on such a paradigm.

But, according to the Ponemon Institute's Larry Ponemon, there is another problem. Ponemon points out that many organizations take the decision to go to the Cloud, and even subscribe to a specific Cloud service provider, without consulting in-house IT professionals, and with little thought to security. The p&l is everything. "The security people are out of the loop," comments Ponemon. "A lot of the companies we talk to don't even talk to their CISOs (Chief Information Security Officers) about moves to the Cloud."

At the same time, says Lieberman, "Cloud providers are not going to provide security until customers demand it, and it becomes a roadblock to revenue. It is a chicken-and-the-egg problem: Cloud providers don't want to provide security and large companies don't want to deploy it."

Lieberman's study reveals something else that is quite interesting, and startling. The fear of Orwell's "Big Brother."

Get this: Almost half (48 percent) of IT pros fear keeping sensitive data in the Cloud because of possible government intervention and/or legal action. "If a government or official body wanted to see what data a company was holding in the Cloud, the Cloud host involved would be legally obliged to provide them with access," says Lieberman. "This means there is very limited privacy in Cloud environments. IT managers know it is much easier to hide data within their own private networks."

Agh yes. Yet another group to be consulted before an organizational move to the Cloud: *the ever-present lawyers*. CEOs and CIOs take note.

Cloud Study with Two Figures, Albert Bierstadt, 1830-1902.

Rudiments

Hackers are breaking into systems for profit. Before, it was about intellectual curiosity and pursuit of knowledge and thrill, and now hacking is big business.

– **Kevin Mitnick**, once the most-wanted cyber-criminal in the United States, today the head of Mitnick Security Consulting

Not long ago, clients of Cloud services provider GoGrid received the following (very disturbing) message: "In the normal process of reviewing our system activity, our Security Team discovered that an unauthorized third party may have viewed your account information, including payment card data. We immediately took action to protect our customers, including notifying federal law enforcement authorities, who have since seized the computing equipment and records of the single individual suspected of this misconduct. The criminal investigation is ongoing, and we will continue to assist the authorities in working toward a successful prosecution."

"SaaS (software as a service) and PaaS (platform as a service) providers all trumpet the robustness of their systems, often claiming that security in the Cloud is tighter than in most enterprises," comments a writer for *ComputerWeekly*. "But the simple fact is that every security system that has ever been breached was once thought infallible. Google was forced to make an embarrassing apology ... when its Gmail service collapsed in Europe, while Salesforce.com is still smarting from a phishing attack ... which duped a staff member into revealing passwords. While Cloud service providers face similar security issues as other sorts of organizations, analysts warn that the Cloud is becoming particularly attractive to cyber crooks."

"The richer the pot of data, the more Cloud service providers need to do to protect it," says IDC research analyst David Bradshaw.

"At the heart of Cloud infrastructure is this idea of multi-tenancy and decoupling between specific hardware resources and applications," explains Datamonitor senior analyst Vuk Trifkovic. "In the jungle of multi-tenant data, you need to trust the Cloud provider that your information will not be exposed."

"For their part," continues the commentator for *ComputerWeekly*, "companies need to be vigilant, for instance about how passwords are assigned, protected and changed. Cloud service providers typically work with numbers of third parties, and customers are advised to gain information about those companies which could potentially access their data."

IDC's Bradshaw says an important measure of security often overlooked by companies is how much downtime a Cloud service provider experiences. He insists that companies should ask to see service providers' reliability reports to determine whether these meet the requirements of the business. He adds that exception-monitoring systems represent another important area which companies should ask their service providers about and document.

One of the world's largest technology companies, Google, has invested a lot of money into the Cloud space, where it recognizes that having a reputation for security is a key determinant of success. "Security is built into the DNA of our products," says a company spokesperson. "Google practices a defense-in-depth security strategy, by architecting security into our people, process and technologies".

All leading Cloud Computing providers agree on the need to develop common standards that address issues such as security and data portability in the Cloud – but they often disagree on how to do this, and use the debate to jockey for the best competitive position.

ComputerWorld's Patrick Thibodeau writes: "The early push for standards is beginning to resemble a NASCAR race – everyone is driving on the same track but sitting in different cars. Multiple organizations are in pursuit of the same checkered flag: a set of standards that will facilitate the adoption of Cloud Computing technologies. The latest organization to join the growing list of standards groups is the IBM-backed Cloud Standards Customer Council, which announced its steering committee [in July 2011]. ... [the] Cloud Standards Customer Council members include Citigroup, Costco Wholesale and Deere & Company."

Meanwhile, the Intel-backed Open Data Center Alliance includes such clients as BMW, Deutsche Bank, J. P. Morgan Chase, Marriott International, Shell and Disney Internet Labs. Overseas companies with seats on the alliance's steering committee include China Life, a Beijing-based insurance company, and China Unicom, a government-owned telecommunications company.

And then we have the Google-backed Cloud Security Alliance, boasting a membership list which includes Coca-Cola and eBay.

"Our intention is to be extremely collaborative with all the various organizations that spawn out there," says Marvin Wheeler, chief strategy officer at Cloud vendor Terremark and chairman of the Open Data Center Alliance. It remains to be seen whether this essentially competitive approach to standards development can lead to genuine, useful consensus in the near term.

Ten Fundamentals of Cloud Computing Security

"The Cloud is here to stay, and the fear and uncertainty associated with any new technology is distracting organizations from securely adopting this IT resource," writes *eWeek's* Chris Preimesberger. "It's not hard to imagine how a newer technology could introduce more security woes; after all, we are constantly seeing news about the latest breaches across the media. However, if we look closely at recent events, the attacks and breaches which build such fear in our minds are often the result of a lack of focus on security fundamentals, not necessarily sophisticated attacks. This is not to say that such attacks can't occur, but the reality is that attackers often focus on the easiest attack route and not the hardest to implement. A criminal will almost always enter a house when no one is home and the door is left open before breaking into a home with the door locked and lights on. When moving IT to the Cloud, organizations need to consider basic security practices analogous to locking the door on their homes."

Harold Moss, CTO of Cloud Security Strategy at IBM, elucidates ten key Cloud Security fundamentals which execs should make sure their IT staffs include in any and every Cloud implementation.

First of all, Moss insists that *foundational controls* lay at the core of any worthwhile security philosophy. They represent maybe 60 security controls (or less), which protect the assets your organization values most. Focusing on them will ensure that as your business embraces Cloud technologies, your approach is consistent with the security controls.

Secondly, he makes the point that security in the Cloud – and an organization's confidence in that security – directly correlate to workload. Each workload has unique considerations, such as regulatory factors and user dependencies. By focusing on the workload and not solely the Cloud IT, you can implement a focused security program with the potential to offer more security than traditional implementations.

Further, Moss explains that organizations must build consensus on security approaches early in the development process. All too often, Cloud technology is adopted without buy-in from all parties. As a result, important security details may be omitted, which can lead to integration and usability challenges. Successful Cloud security implementations require key stakeholders to be aware of and agree upon benefits and challenges.

According to Moss, organizations must as well clearly define and implement a *risk mitigation plan*. Cloud adoption often involves a number of parties, both internal and external. Organizations should adopt a documented risk mitigation plan to allow administrators and staff to rapidly deal with issues in the Cloud. This plan should include not only documentation of risk, and responses to those risks, but also education and training.

Moss's fifth rule states that organizations must not forget *image management* as a security issue. Many Clouds leverage virtualization capabilities. Organizations should implement a storage image management process, which ensures that only appropriate images are actively available. It's also important that all deployed images are correctly identified and managed to prevent image sprawl.

Moss emphasizes the importance of a carefully conducted *security evaluation*. Clouds are complex. Prior to migrating to Cloud technologies, organizations should first evaluate applications and infrastructure for vulnerabilities and ensure that all security controls are in place and operating properly. Ethical hacking is a secondary activity which organizations should use to check their Cloud applications for common vulnerabilities.

Most importantly, Moss recommends that firms take advantage of *commercial security services*. New security services have entered the market that allow organizations to achieve best-of-breed security without the usual overhead. Areas such as intrusion prevention, access and identity management, and security event log management present opportunities for organizations to achieve security goals without putting a strain on existing resources.

Moss goes on to strongly recommend the development of a *resiliency program*. As organizations adopt Cloud-based technologies, they should also look at their resiliency needs. No technology is perfect and the same goes for the Cloud. Make sure that workloads, which are critical to the business, can be rapidly restored in the event of a catastrophe or attack. Be careful to ensure that workloads can be readily restored with minimal impact on business continuity.

Moss also emphasizes the importance of *performance monitoring*. Failing to properly monitor Cloud implementations can result in performance, satisfaction and security issues. Implement an active monitoring program that identifies any threats to the success of the Cloud implementation.

Lastly, Moss says organizations should follow a *Cloud lifecycle model*. Security in general is not a point-in-time statement, but more of an ongoing effort to keep the bad guys out while letting the good guys work. Organizations must be diligent in managing Cloud technologies and in regularly reviewing security.

Changing Your IT Staff's Mindset, Understanding Insider Threats, and Other Things That Go Bump in the Dark

Moving to a Cloud-based platform requires a major change in mindset for IT security professionals.

Traditional defense-in-depth security includes physical security, anti-virus software, firewalls, identity and authorization systems and "DMZ" perimeter networks. But you can't apply these traditional defense-in-depth security precautions directly to public Cloud Computing. Why? Well, most of these systems will be outside your control. Nevertheless, you should still apply the principal of multi-layered security. Furthermore, and most importantly, you should thoroughly examine the security systems and procedures of CSPs (Cloud Service Providers) you are considering.

In short, security for the Cloud simply does not map directly with trad on-premises approaches. Still, despite the differences in approaches, you should nevertheless b e sure to target security levels for the Cloud that are at least as high as those gained from existing on-premises procedures.

In a Cloud-based paradigm, regardless of whether the platform is private or public, you will be working within in an abstracted, virtualized environment. The platform or software may well run atop a shared internally-managed physical infrastructure (as in a Private Cloud) or on one provided by the CSP (as in a Public Cloud). In either scenario, the security architecture used by applications must move up from the platform infrastructure to the application layers.

For example, if a Software as a Service (SaaS) app is provided by a CSP, you've got no control over the platform or infrastructure and you will need to consider and apply all available and/or necessary security controls at the application level. In this instance, the level and robustness of security controls you can deploy will be defined by the CSP. In Private Cloud environments, you are responsible for all levels of security but have more freedom to do what you wish.

Private Clouds might at first seem advantageous over Public Clouds since perimeter security mechanisms are robustly available and completely under your control. However, this advantage may be something of a mirage. Remember that the greatest and highest impact breaches usually occur internally (insider attacks), occurring on the corporate side of the firewall, *behind* network-centric security devices.

Given this, the Cloud-based architecture should be viewed as an chance to protect against *all* threats (not just outsider attacks) by assessing and designing a security paradigm that places emphasis not only on perimeter security, but throughout the whole stack. Take the approach that *all* networks are untrusted. If you start there, the security you design for your new Cloud solution will be the most robust possible, and highly-tuned to threat landscape enterprises are forced to deal with today.

With reference to the above, Moss notes: "The outdated concepts of yesterday's security model focused on building walls around data to keep 'the bad guys' from gaining entry. But today, organizations realize they also face threats from within. In just the last year, nearly half of all breaches were caused by insiders – either by accident or malice."

Whatever the nature of your Cloud architecture – public, private, or hybrid – you must write *all* applications with security first and foremost in mind. Applications must be designed in such a way that: (1) They expose a reduced attack surface. (2) They run with least privilege. (3) They validate all inputs. (4) They require user authentication. (5) They enforce rigid authorization policies. (6) They encrypt data on disk. (7) They likewise encrypt data over the network. (8) And they encrypt data at the client application level.

This recipe – which is sometimes referred to as the *Security Development Lifecycle* (SDL) – describes a strong and absolutely essential methodology for writing any application destined to move to a Cloud-based infrastructure. Enforce these practices and the risks of adopting a Cloud deployment will be sharply minimized. Through this process, you become far less dependent on network based security, which may only be of nominal value in guarding against stealth-based attackers who concentrate on entering without disturbing such controls.

Computer Security Organizations

I've already noted the three primary security organizations working (somewhat cooperatively, but mostly competitively) to develop guidelines and protocols. In the following chapters, I'll give more details on these organizations and their efforts, as well as a useful new tool available free from Microsoft.

Cloud Shadows, Winslow Homer, 1836-1910.

Cloud Security Alliance, the CSA GRK Stack, and STAR

My model for business is the Beatles. They were four guys who kept each others' kind of negative tendencies in check. They balanced each other, and the total was greater than the sum of the parts. That's how I see business: Great things in business are never done by one person. They're done by a team of people.

– Steve Jobs

Founded in 2009, the Cloud Security Alliance (CSA) is a not-for-profit organization that promotes the use of best practices for providing security assurance within Cloud Computing environments.

"The very nature of how businesses use information technology is being transformed by the 'on-demand' Cloud Computing model," said eBay Chief Information Security Officer Dave Cullinane at the time. "It is imperative that information security leaders are engaged at this early stage to help assure that the rapid adoption of Cloud Computing builds in information security best practices without impeding the business. I am proud to be a co-founder of this important initiative."

Another comment from the launch event: "We expect a great deal of migration towards Cloud Computing within the federal government in addition to the already robust Private sector growth," said former White House adviser Paul Kurtz, partner with Good Harbor Consulting, LLC, and Cloud Security Alliance founding member. "The growth of the Cloud should not outpace our ability to protect the data that goes into it, and the Cloud Security Alliance is a key collaborative effort to help assure that is the case."

In mid November of 2011, the CSA released the third version of its *Security Guidance for Critical Areas of Focus in Cloud Computing*. The effort provides a roadmap for organizations wanting to adopt Cloud initiatives securely.

A key update in Version Three is that the domains have been rewritten to enhance security, stability and privacy, guaranteeing corporate privacy in a multi-tenant environment. In addition, the guidelines include a new domain for security-as-a-service.

"Cloud technologies and the adoption of Cloud-based computing and standards have grown tremendously in the two years since the publication of our previous version of the Guidance," says Archie Reed, chief technologist for Cloud security at Hewlett-Packard and one of the three editors of the guidelines "The thinking on Cloud – the tools and the techniques – has evolved significantly, and Version 3 provides the latest best practices to meet today's challenges while demystifying the concept of Cloud services."

The new version – for the 2013 release is indeed the "new" version – "is a significant overhaul of a huge body of work, needed to keep up with the rapidly changing landscape of Cloud technologies and challenges," says Jim Reavis, CSA co-founder and executive director.

Cloud Security Alliance GRC Stack

The Cloud Security Alliance's Governance, Risk Management and Compliance (GRC) Stack delivers an elegant toolkit for enterprises, Cloud providers, IT auditors, security solution providers, and all other major stakeholders to test and assess both Private and Public Clouds against industry-established security best practices, standards and critical compliance rules.

Achieving GRC goals involves meeting carefully defined assessment criteria, demonstrably relevant control objectives and real-time access to necessary supporting data. Whether implementing Private, Public or Hybrid Clouds, the shift to compute-as-a-service contains serious new challenges across the range of GRC requirements.

Available for free download from Cloudsecurityalliance.org, The *Cloud Security Alliance GRC Stack* comprises an integrated suite of four CSA initiatives: CloudAudit, Cloud Controls Matrix, Consensus Assessments Initiative Questionnaire and the CloudTrust Protocol.

CloudAudit provides a common interface and namespace allowing Cloud providers to automate the Audit, Assertion, Assessment, and Assurance (A6) of IaaS, PaaS and SaaS environments and allow authorized consumers of their services to do the same. This is accomplished via an open, extensible, secure interface and methodology. CloudAudit provides the technical foundation to enable transparency and trust in Private and Public Cloud systems.

The Cloud Security Alliance *Cloud Controls Matrix* (CCM) provides fundamental security protocols and principles to help Cloud vendors and and Cloud customers assess the overall security risk of a Cloud provider. CCM delivers a controls framework which enables detailed understanding of the security concepts and principles in synch with the Cloud Security Alliance guidance in 13 domains.

The foundations of Cloud Security Alliance CCM are its compatibility with other industry-standard security guidelines, regulations, and controls frameworks such as the HITRUST CSF, ISO 27001/27002, ISACA COBIT, PCI, HIPAA and NIST.

As a framework, the CCM provides organizations with important structure, detail and clarity relating to information security. CCM adds strength to in-place information security control environments, identifies and reduces consistent security vulnerabilities and threats, and goes a long way toward normalizing security expectations, Cloud terminology and taxonomy, and overall security practices for the Cloud.

The Cloud Security Alliance *Consensus Assessments Initiative* (CAI) was launched to facilitate research, create tools and forge partnerships to enable Cloud Computing assessments. The goal here is enunciate uniform industry-accepted procedures to document what security controls exist in various IaaS,

PaaS, and SaaS offerings, thus providing security control transparency throughout the industry.

This effort has been carefully designed to integrated with and support other projects being implemented by CSA research partners. The first deliverable from this project is the Consensus Assessments Initiative Questionnaire (CAIQ). Available in spreadsheet format, CAIQ provides a set of questions a Cloud consumer and Cloud auditor should be sure to ask of a Cloud provider. CAIQ contains a series of "yes or no" control assertion questions which can be customized to suit each Cloud customer's unique evidentiary requirements.

Finally, the *CloudTrust Protocol* (CTP) provides a precisely-defined mechanism by which Cloud service consumers may ask for and receive information about elements of transparency as applied to individual Cloud service providers. The primary purpose of the CTP is to gather evidence-based confidence that everything that is stated to be happening in the Cloud is indeed happening as claimed – *and nothing else*. When thus assured, Cloud consumers should become more confident to bring more sensitive data and important business functions to the Cloud. With the CTP, Cloud consumers gain a reliable, fast-track way to ascertain important information regarding the compliance, security, privacy, integrity, and operational security history of all service elements performed under the auspices of a given Cloud provider.

These four key initiatives are designed to provid out-of-the-box integration. CloudAudit incorporates the Cloud Controls Matrix as an included namespace. Meanwhile, he Consensus Assessments Initiative Questionnaire has been designed to identify the presence or lack of CCM controls and other key practices defined in the CSA guidance.

Cloud Consumer Advocacy Questionnaire and Information Survey

We recently saw the release of results for the CDC's Cloud Data Governance (CDG) working group's *Cloud Consumer Advocacy Questionnaire and Information Survey*. The survey is the first deliverable for the CDG working group, which now turns its focus to developing best practices recommendations, and prioritizing and responding-to the key problems and questions identified by survey participants.

The questionnaire asked Cloud services consumers to provide their input on the current state of Public Cloud provider maturity in addressing the following key issues: data discovery, location of the data, data aggregation and inference, commingling data with other Cloud customers, use of data security controls, encryption and key management practices, data backup and recovery schemes for recovery and restoration, and data permanence/persistence.

"Cloud Computing shifts the emphasis from 'systems' to 'data', and as a result, stakeholders need to be aware of the best practices for governing and operating data and information in the Cloud," says Ryan Ko, one of the co-chairs of the CDG working group. "With this initial survey, we aimed to capture the current state of data governance and data security capabilities offered by leading Cloud service providers. These results will be extremely useful for our future guidance and research on best practices for data governance and security in the Cloud."

The group surveyed almost 50 experts in senior tech roles at organizations including the industry's largest Cloud providers worldwide. In addition to the survey results, the initial paper also provides working group recommendations, these to be expanded upon in future work products.

"Standardization of data governance policies for Cloud environments will accelerate rapid adoption of Cloud Computing across the industry," says John

Maddison, VP, Executive General Manager Data Center Business Unit of Trend Micro, sponsors of the initiative. "We congratulate the working group on the results of this tremendous undertaking, and look forward to the future work products, which will build on these findings to help consumers gain greater awareness of the best practices for governing and operating data and information in the Cloud."

Security Trust and Assurance Registry (STAR), and the Need for Standardized Metrics

Google, Verizon, Intel, McAfee, Microsoft and Savvis have joined a voluntary program set up by the CSA providing public information about whether contributors comply with CSA-recommended Cloud-security procedures.

By reading reports submitted to CSA's *Security Trust and Assurance Registry* (STAR), potential customers of participating providers can more easily assess whether specific products and services meet their security needs.

Looking to expand its program, CSA is encouraging businesses to require that any Cloud vendors they deal with to submit reports to CSA STAR – and many are doing so.

"For example," notes *ComputerWorld's* Tim Greene, "eBay is requiring the submissions from all Cloud vendors it works with, says the company's CISO Dave Cullinane. He says the information will help eBay security and its customers' privacy. Similarly, Sallie Mae will look for Cloud vendors to demonstrate their security via CSA STAR filings."

"When deploying Security as a Service in a highly regulated industry or environment," says the CSA's latest Guidance for Critical Areas of Focus in Cloud Computing, "agreement on the metrics defining the service level required to achieve regulatory objectives should be negotiated in parallel with the SLA documents defining service."

According to the CSA, topics of particular concern here include identity and access management, data loss protection, Web and email security, encryption and, of course, intrusion prevention.

Summer Clouds, Maine, Charles Allen Curtis, 1886 -1950.

Open Data Center Alliance (and Cooperation with CSA)

ODCA is a customer-focused organization defining requirements to speed delivery of Cloud computing benefits worldwide. Our work helps member companies set strategies to get maximum value from the transition to Cloud, and effectively plan and procure next-generation data center technologies, Cloud infrastructure, and Cloud services. We are paving the way for providers to deliver relevant products for a broad Cloud computing market based on standards developed by collaborative industry organizations. You're cordially invited to engage with other global IT leaders who are sharing knowledge and ideas – working together to create a Cloud computing future that will benefit us all.

– Mario Müeller, ODCA Chairman of the Board and Secretary

"In October [2010]," writes Forrester researcher Richard Fichera, "with great fanfare, the Open Data Center Alliance unfurled its banners. The ODCA is a consortium of approximately 50 large IT consumers, including large manufacturing, hosting and telecomm providers, with the avowed intent of developing standards for interoperable Cloud Computing. In addition to the roster of users, the announcement highlighted Intel with an ambiguous role as a technology adviser to the group. The ODCA believes that it will achieve some weight in the industry due to its estimated $50 billion per year of cumulative IT purchasing power, and the trade press was full of praises for influential users driving technology as opposed to allowing rapacious vendors such as HP and IBM to drive users down proprietary paths that lead to vendor lock-in."

Largely initiated and sponsored by Intel, this organization is essentially designed to push Intel's *Cloud 2015* vision. This vision can be summarized as: (1) creating a federated Cloud where enterprises can share data between internal and external resources, (2) automatically securing applications and resources, (3) improving energy efficiency, and (4) building client-aware-Clouds that will recognize your device and adjust accordingly.

ODCA membership has quadrupled since the founding, and represents more than $100 billion in annual collective IT spend.

Importantly, ODCA and CSA have begun to cooperate in several areas.

Initial collaboration engagements include alignment of the ODCA's Cloud Security Assurance and Monitoring usage models with CSA's Cloud Audit specification and STAR (Security, Trust, and Registry) program.

"As Cloud adoption continues at a rapid pace, we welcome this alignment of ODCA's customer definitions with our best-practices," says the CSA's Jim Reavis. "In addition, we believe certification is a crucial step in growing awareness and implementation of these best-practices among organizations. We are very pleased that ODCA members will be participating in our CCSK certification program, driving deeper understanding and adoption of these best-practices within their organizations."

The organizations have also announced the ODCA's participation in CSA's CCSK (Certification of Cloud Security Knowledge) program, including ODCA representation on CSA's certification board and ODCA member participation in certification testing.

Cloud World, Maynard Dixon, 1875-1946.

Microsoft's Free Cloud Security Readiness Tool

Forewarned, forearmed; to be prepared is half the victory.

– Miguel de Cervantes

Announced in October of 2012, Microsoft's Cloud Security Readiness Tool CSRT) is configured to to aid firms with up to 500 employees assess the likely impact (beneficial or otherwise) of adopting various Cloud-based security services.

CSFT is also meant to help enterprises decide whether or not to go to the Cloud in the first place, or to keep all computing on-premises.

"When we talk to the companies who have not adopted Cloud, 44 percent raised security concerns," says Microsoft's Jeff Jones, director of the firm's Trusted Computing Group. "We then asked what would help them to overcome those concerns, and they called for better use of industry-standards, plus they were looking for a high level of transparency, so they could better understand what they were getting."

Jones continues: "We are approaching this from the perspective of two high-level questions. They need to understand where they are today with respect to security and compliance. Second, if they adopt Cloud security offerings, will I be better off?"

In partnership with such groups as the Cloud Security Alliance, Microsoft has crafted an efficient bundle of recommended strategies and standards. These best practices have in turn been condenced into an efficient tool comprised of just 27 questions. These questions have been precisely designed to provide a paradigm in which to assess an organization's specific needs and status, this leading to a set of expert recommendations for how to improve existing security policies, technologies and procedures either in or out of the Cloud.

CSRT is available free of charge.

CSRT is customizable to a range of vertical markets, fitting to the changing standards applicable to each. In essence, CSRT measures "security maturity" in 10 key areas, such as architecture, human resources security, facilities security, info security, data governance, legal, release management, risk management, and resiliency and operational management.

Within each area, the tool provides enterprises with an easy work-through paradigm which results in a report of about 60 pages describing their current state and recommending what to do next to improve security in particular areas.

"So it provides recommended mitigation, and it also describes what benefits you would get from adopting Cloud-based security," says Jones.

Detail of ethereal clouds from *The Voyage of Life* by Hudson River School artist Thomas Cole, 1801-1848.

Cloud Standards Customer Council, and the Question: Which Standards Organization Will Prevail?

The most serious mistakes are not being made as a result of wrong answers. The truly dangerous thing is asking the wrong question.

– Peter Drucker

The nonprofit industry association Object Management Group (OMG) formed the Cloud Standards Customer Council (CSCC) in April of 2011 with major backing from IBM as well as CA, Rackspace, Software AG and Kaavo. Among end users are Lockheed Martin, Citigroup, North Carolina State University and more than 40 other organizations. The CSCC is a user advocacy group dedicated to accelerating the successful adoption of the Cloud, with a focus on standards, interoperability and security and issues involved with moving to the Cloud. Its stated ambition is to "complement existing Cloud standards efforts and develop a set of client-driven requirements to give Cloud users the same choices, flexibility, and openness they have with traditional IT environments."

"The Cloud Standards Customer Council [brings together] Cloud veterans [so that they might] discover and disseminate best practices for moving to and managing the Cloud and help to drive standards across industry, both to end-users and vendors to bring down costs and increase choice," says Richard Mark Soley, Ph.D., chairman and CEO, OMG.

Founding members seem enthusiastic.

Angel Diaz, vice president, IBM Software Standards, comments: "Ultimately, this effort is about how organizations can use what they have today and extend their business – using open standards – to get the greatest benefits from Cloud."

"End users confront the challenges of implementing Cloud on a daily basis. The Cloud Standards Customer Council will bring together these Cloud veterans into a community where they can discover and disseminate best practices for moving to and managing the Cloud and help to drive standards across industry, both to end-users and vendors to bring down costs and increase choice," says Soley.

"To make Open Cloud successful and reflective of real business needs, IBM is asking for client feedback regarding their direction and priorities around Cloud standards development," continues Diaz. "This council is designed to focus on the reality of what provides the greatest Cloud Computing benefits for clients."

"We are thrilled to work with the Cloud Standards Customer Council and leading global organizations to help drive customer requirements into the development of industry standards for Cloud Computing," states Jamal Mazhar, Founder and CEO of Kaavo. "With perspective from the changing Cloud landscape and by collaborating with CSCC, we can help shape best practices that result in real-world value for thousands of companies."

"Rackspace is always working to create new ways to gain customers feedback so we can provide fanatical support. The Cloud standards customer council provides us a venue to follow customers leads on the open Cloud," says Mark Interrante, Vice President Cloud Products, Rackspace.

So, Which Standards Organization Will Prevail?

As noted, the Cloud Standards Customer Council is backed by IBM, allowing for some strong business buy-in. But the same thing applies to the Open Data

Center Alliance – supported by Intel, with big-name members such as BMW, Deutsche Bank, Shell and Marriott. Likewise the Google-backed Cloud Security Alliance, whose membership list includes Coca-Cola and eBay.

Not all of the new standards are likely to survive. But which ones will? As far as the Open Data Center Alliance is concerned, market leadership determines the survival chances of Cloud standards. According to the Open Data Center Alliance, its membership represents more than 100 billion dollars in annual ICT spending power. It wouldn't surprise this writer to see at least a large section of the market embrace the standards that these big ICT spenders are designing for the Cloud.

Sunset Across the Hudson Valley by Hudson River School
artist Frederic Edwin Church, 1826-1900.

Federal Risk and Authorization Management Program (FedRAMP)

Bureaucracy is a giant mechanism operated by pygmies.

– Honore de Balzac

As of mid-December 2011, the United States federal government launched an assessment and monitoring program which insists Cloud providers achieve a certain level of security before being allowed to work with the federal government.

The Federal Risk and Authorization Management Program (FedRAMP) sets clearly-defined security baselines for contractors seeking to the federal government with Cloud services. Over two years in development, FedRAMP is a "first step" toward securing Cloud environments, according to Federal CIO Steven VanRoekel.

The federal government spends hundreds of millions of dollars securing its IT systems, and much of the tasks are "duplicative, inconsistent and time consuming," according to VanRoekel. FedRAMP's "do once, use many times" framework is designed to save money and time, and minimize staff required to conduct security assessments. VanRoekel estimates there will be a 30 percent to 40 percent cost savings for the government while securing Cloud services under FedRAMP. "FedRAMP enables agencies to deploy Cloud technologies, while realizing efficiencies of scale to substantially reduce costs and transition time," he wrote on the White House blog.

Starting in June of 2012, all federal agencies have been required to use FedRAMP when evaluating and purchasing "commercial and non-commercial Cloud services that are provided by information systems that support the operations and assets of the departments and agencies," according to a memo from VanRoekel. The requirement covers systems that are provided or managed by other departments or agencies, contractors, or other sources, VanRoekel adds. Because vendors will already be certified under FedRAMP, agencies will be able to move through the procurement process more easily, swiftly and economically. Along with a set of minimum security controls Cloud providers have to meet, FedRAMP also defines a continuous monitoring tool that all agencies are required to use.

Officials from the Department of Defense, Homeland Security and the General Services Administration oversee the FedRAMP authorization board. The board will define and update the security authorization requirements and approve accreditation criteria for third-party organizations that will assess Cloud providers for FedRAMP compliance. GSA will also create service-level agreements and templates for the program and establish a record repository to house and securely share assessment, accreditation and authorization information across agencies.

"Federal agency adoption of the Cloud is inevitable. The only question is if it will be done in a secure or insecure fashion. The FedRAMP program could be the game-changer in this equation," notes TechAmerica VP Jennifer Kerber.

"The FedRAMP baseline Cloud security controls are grounded in FISMA standards and are applicable to both Cloud and non-Cloud security controls and guidance. There are no 'new' controls for FedRAMP," says David McClure, associate administrator for the Office of Citizen Services and Innovative Technologies at the General Services Administration (GSA). "However, the FedRAMP baseline does use selected controls above the existing low or moderate impact NIST baseline that address specific characteristics of Cloud computing, including multitenancy, shared resource pooling, lack of trust, visibility, and control of the service provider's infrastructure. ... Operationally, FedRAMP will evolve as a program to reflect the changing nature of Cloud computing and incorporate lessons learned. As Cloud computing, standards and capabilities evolve, so will FedRAMP."

The directive not only addresses security standards, but also includes several measures designed to facilitate the implementation of those standards in the acquisition and contracting process. For example, GSA will be required to develop templates that can satisfy FedRAMP security authorization requirements through standard contract language and service level agreements (SLAs) for use in the acquisition of Cloud services.

Importantly, vendors of Cloud services will be required to obtain approval of their offerings by a third- party assessment organization. These organizations will perform initial and periodic assessment of the products and services offered by CSPs regarding FedRAMP requirements. The third-party organizations will provide evidence of compliance, and play an ongoing role in ensuring that CSPs meet security standards.

GSA has also set up a Program Management Office to facilitate implementation of FedRAMP that will include a central repository of CSP security authorization packages that executive departments and agencies can use with their Cloud migrations. However, even with the establishment of baseline security standards in FedRAMP, vendors will still have to be nimble in executing contracts with federal agencies, since requirements are bound to change over time.

As of this writing (February 2013), most organizations are finding FedRAMP to be a rather steep thing to ascend.

Of the more than 80 Cloud providers who have thus far attempted to receive FedRAMP certification, less than half are ready to pass the process. So says Kathy Conrad, who serves principal deputy associate administrator with the General Services Administration's Office of Citizen Services and Innovative Technologies.

FedRAMP, the Federal Risk Authorization Management Program, is based upon trust. "The essence of that trust," Conrad insists, "is the rigor and the integrity of its security assessment that then can be leveraged across government." Conrad goes on to say that FedRAMP was intentionally designed to be quite a rigorous process, and will never be dumbed-down.

At this writing only a total of two Cloud providers have been able to win provisional approval under FedRAMP – Autonomic Resources LLC and the much larger CGI Federal, a subsidiary of CGI Group, Inc.

Lockheed Martin and other major government contractors? They're still working on it. Stay tuned.

About the Author

Lars Nielsen has more than thirty years experience as a systems developer and administrator for a range of Fortune 500 companies. Nielsen is the author of New Street's popular *Computing: A Business History* and the bestselling *Little Book of Cloud Computing,* updated annually. He is also co-author of New Street's bestselling *A Simple Introduction to Data Science.* He resides in Amsterdam.

Also of Interest

The Little Book of Cloud Computing, 2013 Edition (Including Coverage of Big Data Tools) by Lars Nielsen

Computing: A Business History by Lars Nielsen

A Simple Introduction to Data Science by Lars Nielsen and Noreen Burlingame

About the Publisher

New Street Communications, LLC publishes and distributes superior works of nonfiction (and, through our Dark Hall Press imprint, select fiction in the Horror genre). We are a *digital-native* imprint. As such, we primarily make our titles available as eBooks, though often in paper editions as well. In the nonfiction we cover the intersection of digital technology and society; transformative business communication and innovation (particularly the conceptualizing of elegant new tools, markets, products and paradigms); socially-relevant childrens' literature; and literary criticism. New Street's nonfiction books are authored by distinguished scholars, journalists, entrepreneurs, developers and thought leaders.

newstreetcommunications.com

www.ingramcontent.com/pod-product-compliance
Lightning Source LLC
Chambersburg PA
CBHW061036050326
40689CB00012B/2862